From Star Performer

to

Corporate Tiger

5 Key Skills to Succeed for New Managers

Manu Sharma

Contents

Preface

The book you have in your hand is intended to provide New Managers with practical advice and tips to develop and hone 5 key skills to succeed as managers. The skills shared in this book will be useful throughout your career. There is no particular order recommended to read the book you can start from the skill which interest you more or just learn the skills as they are introduced in the chapter.

This book is the culmination of my learnings from my professional career spanning over 25 years. I had the opportunity of working at different levels and functional areas. As part of my job I was interacting with academicians, consultants and director and CEO of various Multinational organizations in the country, their advice, guidance and support helped me to evolve as a Manager.

I was also engaged with an institute which imparted training courses to enhance the managerial and leadership skills of diploma engineers. As part of my engagement I was closely involved with more than 1500 diploma engineer going through their career transformation journey. Some of them witnessed spiral growth whereas others could achieve only moderate results. I was able to identify key skills which helped them to achieve the quantum jump in their career.

In the corporate environment it is common for an individual to get promoted as Managerial level on the bases of their past performance and experience. Supervising a talented and diverse team poses a challenge for which New Manager are not equipped. They have to plan and strategize to enable their team to achieve organizational goals. Since plans and strategies are not set in stone, the things may not move as planned and people may not respond as expected. Question disturbing the Manager in this situation is that should they micro manage their teams or should they give team full autonomy to their teams. Managers have to improvise and adapt to the demands of the situation. This book will give you a heads up for developing key skills to succeed as a New Manager and equip you to handle such situations.

I am sure you will find this book informative and practical and it will provide you the springboard for creating a Successful Career as a Leader.

If you find it helpful you share it with your friends and teammates, as sharing your experience helps you grow. Help me improve and serve the community of first-time managers. You can visit my website www.manusharma.live You will find additional self-help complimentary resources at https://career-boosters.teachable.com/

I would like to express my special thanks to my wife, my son and other family members and friends for their untiring support and inputs for making this book a reality.

Introduction

You've just moved into your new independent office, equipped with your own Mac and your name shining on the door. You have been a Star Performer. You've worked really hard to get here. Now you are the "Manager." Congratulations on your promotion are pouring in, and your confidence, motivation, and morale are at their zeniths. But sooner than later, your bosses' expectations and the job responsibilities start to pull you down. Every time you falter or miss a deadline, you can feel your rival managers snickering, and hear your juniors whispering behind your back. You are confused, finding yourself in the midst of chaos. The chaos follows you everywhere you go. This is the first challenge, which every new manager has to face.

It is common for people who excel in non-management positions to be promoted to management roles. Many such people who get these promotions find the transition from a non-managerial role to a managerial role difficult. They forget that it was their personal skills and expertise which helped them to excel, to distinguish them as Star Performers. But the skills required to be a manager and team leader are altogether different. You must meet set goals by synchronizing the efforts of your team. Meeting your boss's expectations and making erstwhile colleagues take and follow orders from you can be draining. You may have a fear of failure, of disappointing your boss, and of missing deadlines (due to lack of adequate support of the team). Failures in the early days of leadership roles are common. Don't let the pressure of a new role bog you down. You can handle it and can do better. Even seasoned leaders once faced failures, but they learned from their mistakes and became better leaders. If you, as a new manager, are feeling a bit disoriented or confused, believe me: it is normal. Becoming a manager is not the destination. It is the start of new journey. It will be tough but rewarding. This book will help you to adapt faster to your new role and make your journey smoother. I will share the 5 essential skills of a leader which you should develop as a Manager. These skills will help you to become not just a leader, but also a Corporate Tiger.

Managers who are good leaders are always in short supply, whether it is in the field of business, politics, or not-for-profit organizations. First-time managers spend more of their time and effort in getting the job done rather than focusing on their leadership skills. No wonder the research conducted by CEB shows that 60% of new managers fail within the first 24 months, as they lack the formal training to lead and build trust in their team. Leaders have to constantly keep building their skills to lead effectively. This is evident from the data from the Chief Learning Officer Business Intelligence Board, which shows that 94% of learning organizations either plan to increase or keep their level of investment the same in leadership development. As a manager, it is pertinent to acquire leadership skills at the early stages of your managerial career. These skills will not only help you to succeed as a manager, but also help you to become a Corporate Tiger.

The definition of leadership has changed over time and varies by individual. When we hear the word "leader," the names of heads of the state immediately pop into our minds; if you are in a business meeting or conference, the names of successful business leaders will come to mind. These business leaders often hold titles such as CEO, Managing Director, Unit Head, or Branch Head. But the quality of leadership is not exclusive to higher positions or roles in the hierarchy. It is more of a skill and an attitude. Your skill drives the team to achieve goals and your attitude influences and inspires your team to give their best. In my opinion, one who is better than others in the field is a leader. In other words, leadership is subjective. Your environment and your competition bring out the best in you. You keep improving your skills and compete with yourself as a leader. If your actions inspire your co-workers, your juniors, to better their performance, you are a leader in your own right—even if you do not have a title.

As they say: "People don't leave jobs; they leave their bosses." As a New Manager, you do not want people to leave you. You should master the skills required to be an effective leader. Fortunately, anyone can easily learn these skills. In this book, I'll share with you the 5 essential leadership skills. These skills will help you to lead a team successfully and to establish yourself as a Corporate Tiger. I have worked with great bosses, including a Technocrat, an Eye Surgeon Turned Entrepreneur, a Top B-School Graduate, and Bureaucrats. My leadership experience was enriched working with officers of the Indian Army, and two Padma Shri Awardees(fourth highest civilian Honour in India). While working with these diverse bosses, I noticed they all have some skills in common. I assimilated some of their leadership skills, which have helped me to excel in my career. Now I want to share these skills with you, so you too can benefit from them.

The skills that I will share with you are easily learned. You can practice these skills and master them. As a New Manager, you may find yourself in a dilemma: should you delegate, or should you do it yourself? You will have to master the skills of communicating goals and directions, of taking reviews and feedback, of acting on these inputs and responding to trends, and of fine tuning and planning ahead in order to enable the team to reach its goal. Besides the challenges you face in managing the team and its dynamics, you have to motivate your team, make decisions, and keep the team on track. Mastering these skills may not guarantee an immediate success, but it will definitely put you on the fast track for your next promotion.

In this book, our focus is on 5 key leadership skills that, as a New Manager, you should develop. Even if you are not currently in a leadership role, you can master these skills and prepare for future leadership roles. As a first-time manager, you will be facing numerous challenges, such as handling additional job responsibilities and adapting from doing the work yourself to overseeing others doing it. The role is not limited to managing the work; you are also responsible for your team, making decisions, and carrying out the vision and mission of the organization. To prepare yourself for these new responsibilities, practice and hone the skills you learn in this book. These skills will help you make a smooth transition from a Star Performer to a Manager and, eventually, to a Corporate Tiger.

These critical skills are:

- Effective Communication

- Adapting for Growth
- Building a High-Performance Team
- Strategic Thinking and Planning
- The Art of Delegation

I will share these skills with you in detail in the following chapters. You should start practicing them as you progress through the book. Soon, you will master these 5 skills and become a Corporate Tiger.

So let's learn them, practice them, and master them to be an effective leader! Your bosses have recognized your good work and believe you are ready for a larger role. Let's get started!

Skill 1: Effective Communication

****

"Communication is a skill that you can learn. It's like riding a bicycle or typing. If you're willing to work at it, you can rapidly improve the quality of every part of your life."

-Brian Tracy

Communication is the foremost skill of a leader. It is the first skill we learn, even before we learn to speak, and all living beings possess this skill. Nature has empowered each living species with the ability to communicate on some level. Similarly, the skill of communication can differ in each human individual as well. Communication has purpose. Managers communicate to give instructions and orders. Leaders use it to inspire, influence and modulate the behaviors and actions of their team to meet organization goals.

The leaders develop skills to clearly communicate their ideas and visions with their team. Studies show that managers spend 80% of their time communicating. When you receive plans from your seniors, you translate them into targets and action plans for your team to follow, then get feedback reports and relate them to your seniors. As a New Manager, you must master this skill in order to have a competitive edge. Communication skills are paramount. To communicate effectively, you need both clarity of thought and the ability to express ideas and share information with a variety of audiences. Managers practice communication; leaders master the art of effective communication. Communication is merely the expression of an idea. Effective communication, however, is a precise and intentional message aimed at achieving a desired result. New managers have a hard time understanding the difference between communication and effective communication. Here's an example: "We need to finish this report" is just a statement, whereas an effective message is, "We need to finish the sales report by 5:00 PM today." As a New Manager, you should develop the habit of thinking through your communication before you share with the team.

Benefits of effective communication

- Minimizes misunderstandings and confusion
- Ensures that team members know what you expect

- Generates a greater number of ideas
- Increases the chances that you'll reach your goals

I have seen people placing too much emphasis on enunciation, improving the vocabulary, and getting the grammar right as part of preparation for being a leader. But just having command over the language does not make you an effective leader. It is effective communication. Effective communication requires you to listen to and understand your audience. New managers, empowered by the additional authority and responsibility, often forget to listen. Leaders should listen more and speak less to foster clear communication. Unfortunately, high schools and colleges lack adequate focus in teaching the secret to becoming an effective communicator: becoming a good listener. We are seldom taught to understand others and have empathy, especially in engineering colleges. With more and more jobs being replaced by computers and robots equipped with Artificial Intelligence, schools should be equipping students with the essential skills of effective communication, as these are the skills which machines will not be able to replace. The nuance of "effective" separates an average Manager from a Corporate Tiger.

Communicating in everyday words, devoid of any jargon or acronyms, makes it easier for people to understand your goals and expectations. This skill can help you excel irrespective of the field in which you are working. Even if you are technically sound, if you cannot communicate well, your seniors will overlook you for promotion to a leadership role. As a manager, you have to communicate not only with your subordinates, but also with the clients and other stakeholders. An iota of doubt in your message can cost your organization a contract or client.

Influential leaders understand that effective communication is not only about words. Your team notices everything—your words, attitude, and actions make up a complete package. Put simply, communication is not just the words you use, but also your body language and tone, to convey the message. History is full of examples of leaders who are still a source of inspiration not for what they said, but how they lived their life as per their beliefs and philosophy. Communication is the transmission of a message by the sender to the receiver. Ideally, this message should be understood by the receiver as the sender intended. As a leader, you are required to translate the ideas into actions. If your body language does not support your spoken or written message, the message loses its objective. You cannot talk about cost cutting while sitting in a luxury hotel. Mahatma Gandhi and Martin Luther King Jr. are two of the greatest leaders of their times. Both had excellent communication skills. They practiced what they preached. Your behavior conveys your temperament and beliefs regardless of the words you choose. The words will inspire people for a short time, but it is the actions of the leaders which have a lasting impression. In the words of Sam Walton, founder of Walmart and one of the richest men:

"A lot of people think it's crazy of me to fly coach whenever I go on a commercial flight, and maybe I do it a little bit. But I feel like it's up to me as a leader to set an example. It's not fair for me to ride one way and ask everybody else to ride another way. The minute you do that, you start building resentment, and your whole team idea begins to strain at the seams."

Communication reflects a leader's character. It reflects your level of genuineness, seriousness, and commitment. When a leader is all talk and no action, people miss out on the message. In other words, as a manager you should affirm your words with actions, to earn the respect and loyalty of your team. "Walk the Talk." It is said that an effective leader can inspire ordinary people to deliver extraordinary results. But is it true? Yes! Leaders inspire their team to achieve greater heights with their words and actions. It is the way they communicate that gets things done. This has been one of the common attributes of all my bosses. One of my CEOs always used to say, “It is my effective communication skills that have made me what I am today.” You need to learn the language of your audiences, especially the team you are addressing, whether they are your superiors, stakeholders, or clients. Knowing about their background will help you to fine tune your communication to catch their attention and maintain their interest. Top management understands the language of money; the production engineers understand the language of productivity; and the marketing executives will understand the sales targets. No matter how good you are technically, if you cannot communicate in the language the people understand, you will not be able to get their attention. A simple statement like “implementing a new plan will result in improved productivity” may not interest an audience of Top Management members. But a little tinkering may make their heads turn: “Implementing a new plan will result in additional revenue of 1 million per month.” Towards production engineers, we may customize it to something like: “Implementing a new plan will improve productivity by 5%.” And the marketing executives will be interested to hear: “Implementing a new plan will improve sales by 10%.”

You will get nowhere, and always be working in the background, if your communication is not effective enough to get the desired response. But your effective communication will cover up average technical skills. While working with one particular CEO, I witnessed how he converted ordinary messages into inspiring communications, stirring the emotions of the audience to respond appropriately.

The way effective leaders communicate, the words they choose and the emotions they stir, makes the difference. You will find that all the world's greatest leaders are excellent communicators. For communication to happen, you need to create an environment where the flow of ideas is without any barriers.

In an organization, the hierarchy and management levels typically restrict communication. That is one of the barriers to effective communication. Others can be age, your social status and cultural background, and ethnicity. Effective leaders make conscious efforts to remove such virtual barriers. I suggest some actions that you can take as a leader to remove/reduce the barriers to effective communication:

- Build stronger relationships

- Ensure the message is accessible and reaches every employee
- Encourage bottom-up, employee-driven communication
- Listen more and invite more communication

Build stronger relationships

It is your interpersonal skills that are most effective in transferring your emotions, your ideas, and your feelings and in building trust. For healthy interpersonal communication, you need to have strong relationships based on mutual trustworthiness. To build such relationships, you have to show a genuine concern for your team members, your internal and external customers, your suppliers, and your community. A relationship founded on trust is important in order to sustain healthy communication. Without trust, you cannot communicate effectively.

To create an environment of trust, leaders have to build connections with the team and show a genuine concern. This is true even for your personal relationships. Many marriages fail because couples cannot build or sustain trust. When trust is missing, spouses lie to one another, and that leads to more distrust and disappointment. Eventually, a barrier grows up between the couple, and the relationship fails. The same can happen in any relationship between you and others.

In his book 7 Habits of Highly Effective People, Steven Covey elaborates on this concept. He talks about the emotional bank account. Just like a financial bank account, where you make deposits and withdraw funds when needed, you need to invest your trust in the emotional bank account. The currencies in the emotional bank account are courtesy, kindness, honesty, and commitment. These currencies gradually build your emotional bank balance. Discourtesy, disrespect, ignoring, and other threats drain the account. Each dialogue we have with others is a transaction, and has a positive or negative effect on your emotional trust account. As a leader, you should always keep the currencies of emotional banks balanced and use it wisely to build an environment of trust. This will create an environment conducive to effective communication.

The bigger your emotional balance with another person, the better the level of communication. You should not allow your personal biases or company hierarchy to come between you and another. You need to understand that communication goes both ways. As a leader, it's your job to set the tone for interactions within your organization or team by building a powerful bond of trust.

Ensure the message is accessible and reaches every employee

As the organization and the team begin to grow, reaching out to everyone becomes more difficult. It is a challenge to build a communication strategy to disseminate important information to the right people. Despite our advanced communication systems, almost two-thirds of employees feel that they are not told important information. They do not read the emails sent, ignore the notices posted on the notice boards, ignore messages on WhatsApp groups. Drilling down the information to the last level is important. You need a communication strategy to ensure that the right information reaches the right employees at the right time.

A simple strategy is to make the important information easily accessible to the staff. Be transparent in decision-making. This will reduce frustration and encourage a free flow of communication. Searching for information is one major waste of an employee's work hours.

Start an initiative to organize your workplace's information to make it easily accessible, and watch as your team's productivity improves. This will build trust and reduce frustration among employees, as well as have a positive impact on employee engagement, motivation, and productivity.

Encourage bottom-up, employee-driven communication

In an organization, communication typically flows down from the top. The employees are given instructions and are asked to report the progress. In other words, we push instructions and orders from the top on employees lower in the hierarchy, and pull information from the employees in the shape of reports. By the time management pulls information, the damage may already have been done, and the report holds only historic importance. Effective leaders create a communication system that enables employees to provide feedback and participate in the decision-making process. Sam Walton, founder of Walmart, was often seen meeting the truck drivers, as he believed they visited the most stores and could provide substantial information for improving Walmart's operations. Good managers encourage two-way conversations and make employees feel like they can speak up. They encourage a culture of "Yell for Help." If employees drive communication and the focus is on them, we create a two-way communication culture. There are various employee engagement initiatives like suggestion schemes, kaizens that support and engage employees in decision-making. Such initiatives play a big role in improving the overall productivity and motivation of the team. The team becomes proactive in finding solutions to problems rather than waiting for the management to identify and fix them. As a manager, you can work towards developing a platform within the organization for sharing best practices, and reward and recognize the ideas in such a platform.

Listen more and invite more communication

Outstanding leaders have realized that a strong internal communication strategy is important to the success of an organization. More and more organizations are implementing Enterprise Resource Planning (ERP) software to enable free flow of information and improved coordination between departments. But ERP software is just a tool. Leaders inspire and motivate their team by sharing organizational goals and plans. Leaders listen to their team members, showing interest in the challenges they are facing both on the professional and personal fronts to earn their commitment and trust. Less than one-third of new managers are aware of the corporate vision and mission statements, and they are often lost in the daily targets and meetings. This is because they have not been prepared for the role of leadership. To such managers, the Vision and Mission are a fancy slogan displayed at the entry point of the organization. They are never able to inspire and motivate their teams because they themselves are uninspired and unmotivated.

During a training session at one of my client companies, I asked the Senior Manager to explain their vision. He asked a new intern to share it. The intern was well-versed in the vision of the organization and his own role. The CEO of the company addresses all the frontline managers, where he shares the organization's vision and mission and future goals with them. This was one of the most inspiring sessions I had conducted. When I later checked with their HR department, they reported a much better attrition rate than other companies in the region, even when the salaries were at par with the industry standard. The employees want to be involved in the vision and be part of the larger picture. As a leader, aim to have at least a quarterly meeting with your team to figure out what the management needs to do in order to meet the organization's goals. The level of commitment and enthusiasm of the team will result in increased productivity.

The Vision and Mission statements must be reviewed with the team at regular intervals to ensure the goals and the action plans are in accordance.

Tips for Effective Communication

You're using communication skills every time you contact your team or your client. Every phone call, every meeting, every chat, and every email reflects your ability to communicate and keep a finger on the pulse of your organization.

What makes for effective communication?

The hallmarks of good communication are clarity, relevant detail, and honesty. Clarity means that you must be able to tailor your words for the better understanding of your listener. It should be devoid of acronyms and jargon. You're not communicating effectively if the listener or reader can't understand what you need from or expect of them. You should avoid internal contradictions and ensure that the message is in line with previous communications or practices. To avoid any misunderstandings. In case there are any contradictions, they should be clearly mentioned in the message. When passing on instructions, we should explain logically the intent and their importance.

Detail means that you are specific about what you want, expect, or need to know, and when and in what form you require or expect the response or feedback. If you delegate a task and the team member still has questions about what to do or how to do the job, and when and how it is to be completed, you need to sharpen your communication skills. The details should also include any precedence or practice that is being followed, or what is the accepted business rule to be followed.

Honesty means that you are transparent when communicating with your team. That doesn't mean you share with them your perceptions or fears, but it means that you do not mislead them or deliberately omit information that might help them achieve their goals. You share all the information and risks involved. Honesty is a virtue which is expected of the leader at all times. When you are a leader, people observe your actions more closely than you probably realize. Any ambiguity between your actions and words will not go unnoticed, and the next time they will not take your communication at face value.

Here are a few tips for communicating effectively.

- In writing, keep your sentences and paragraphs short.
- Remember, you are writing to communicate, not to impress.
- Use illustrations and examples to drive your point home.
- Read - Redo and repeat to make sure that the information delivered will generate the desired response.
- While speaking, think, think, and think again before you say it.
- Understand your audience before making them understand you.
- Don't use jargon or acronyms unless you're sure they'll understand it.

- Avoid ambiguity in the message.
- Logically justify contradictions or indicate them as exceptions.
- Pay attention to how the listener reacts to what you say.
- Make sure you are facing your audience while speaking.
- Be available to answer team questions and be patient in doing so.
- Evaluate or reevaluate information before passing it on.

Besides the above-mentioned tips, I suggest three tests you can use to check if your message meets the criteria for effective communication. The three tests are:

1. Three R Test
2. Three C Test
3 Five P Test

Each of these tests is applicable at all stages of communication, whether you are planning, developing, or drafting your communication. Here's how each test works.

Three R Test

The Three R Test refers to three elements of communication, which are bound to improve overall effectiveness. The underlying spirit of the test is that the right message, delivered at the right time and using the right medium, can get you the desired results. Under this test you ask three questions:

1. Is it the Right message?
2. Is it the Right Time to Share the message?
3. What will be the Right Medium to deliver the message?

In this test, the most focus is on the timing and medium of the message to be delivered. The relevance of this test has increased with the growth and multiplicity of the channels of communication that exist today. The message has to be customized to suit the medium being used. Moreover, you cannot use just any medium to convey the message. There are certain messages which are formal and contain private or sensitive information. These cannot be sent through an informal medium like Whatsapp or Telegram. Similarly, you have to decide the medium based on the audience for which the message is meant. Some messages are more effective when they are delivered on paper or in a one-on-one setting.

Similarly, when you have a big announcement to make, you must be very particular about the timing of the announcement. You may have come across many companies that plan a product launch or big sale around festival seasons or during holidays. There exist whole marketing campaigns centering around the 4th of July, Christmas, and Halloween. Generally, when you have to announce a big expansion plan or technical innovation, you should plan it around a time when the overall motivation and morale of the employees is expected to be high. Conversely, difficult decisions, sugarcoated or otherwise, can cause a total upheaval if not delivered at the right time.

Speaking of difficult decisions: The right message for communicating hard decisions will have rationale, remorse, and resolution, whereas in a normal message, remorse can be replaced with good conscience. Trust, as we shared earlier in the chapter, is a very important element in any communication. The importance of this test is to check the message, its timing, and the medium of communication so that a trusting relationship is strengthened.

Three C Test

The Three C Test is the second test you should put to your message. The three Cs are often quoted by communication experts and trainers, and are essential elements of any good communication. The three Cs stand for:

1. Clear

2. Concise

3. Correct

A **Clear** message refers to the communication being understandable and straightforward. The message should not contain any jargon, flashy words, or abbreviations. Read the message from the perspective of the reader. Make sure that the message has been written not to impress, but to make the person understand. The intent of any good communication is that the message is received and understood by the receiver as desired by the sender.

A **Concise** message does not mean that it does not carry the necessary details, but that it is free from unnecessary details. The attention span of your audience is shrinking; everyone is hard-pressed for time. Now, as you move up the corporate ladder, you will have audiences with larger egos and shorter attention spans. You need to practice the art of "saying a lot with few words."

A **Correct** message is the heart and soul of any communication. You should check the message so as to ensure that the facts stated in the message are correct, and that there are no grammatical or spelling mistakes. An incorrect communication can do more damage than good.

Five P Test

The Five P Test is another test which you can put to your communication before you send it. This test is inspired by the Noting technique used in many government departments. I have modified this technique a little to make it more conducive to our goal, which is to improve your message. The five Ps in this test stand for:

1. Purpose
2. People
3. Process or Procedure
4. Presumptions
5. Preferred outcome

1. **Purpose**

The first test is to check if your message meets the desired objective for which the communication is being done. As a manager, you might be dealing with multiple issues at the same time, so it is possible you might lose your focus and write without an objective in mind. You must know why you are writing. Is it to inform or to express your feelings, to seek support for a social cause, or to share a plan or a report, or to influence a decision or action of the receiver of your communication? Be clear about why you are making the communication.

2. **People**

People refers to those for whom the communication is meant, or the receiver of your message. Whether you are preparing a speech or writing an email, you must make an effort to understand your audience and keep them in mind while preparing your draft. Use this knowledge to customize your message for their easy understanding. Remember that you are communicating with people, not machines. Make your communication interesting and add emotions in the message. The message should be checked to ensure that it stirs the right kind of emotions in the people receiving the communication.

3. **Procedure**

The procedure to be used for communicating must be kept in mind. The tools or the aids to be used for communication, medium and mode of communication will play an important role in presenting your ideas and thoughts to your reader. In written communication, you have to decide if you are going to send an email or a typed or handwritten letter. At times, we may like to convey the message using visual tools. If the message is verbal, are you going to convey it over the phone, sent as a voice mail, said face-to-face, or presented to a larger audience? The message needs to be fine-tuned according to the procedure of communication.

4. **Presumptions**

Avoid using presumptions in your communication. You should substantiate your suggestions and ideas with some evidence or examples. Back it up with logic and reasoning, and where possible give precedence of similar matters to ease decision-making and support your claim. Another aspect to be looked into in this portion of the test is to ensure that the complete background of the case has been explained and that nothing has been left to the imagination of the receiver.

5. **Preferred outcome**

In the preferred outcome test, check that the message has covered what action is desired from the receiver. It can propose a solution to a problem or suggest a decision, or contain an appeal or a call to action. It conveys to the reader or receiver what he is expected to do after having read the message, and, in case of any inquiries, whom the receiver should contact.

These tips will help to establish you as a powerful and effective communicator and secure favorable responses, and, ultimately, sincere complaisance from your team.

Next, we'll talk about why you must be adaptable in order for your audience to follow you along the path of growth.

Skill 2: Adapting for Growth

****

"Adaptability is not imitation. It means power of resistance and assimilation."

-Mahatma Gandhi

Adaptability is an indispensable skill for a leader. It can be a deciding factor between success and failure in any business. Change is not new to business; it has been there since the time immemorial, only now the pace of change has increased. According to Harvard Business Review, the percentage of companies falling out of the top three rankings in their industry increased from 2% in 1960 to 14% in 2008. The correlation between profitability and market share is also changing. According to calculations by Harvard Business Review, the probability that the market share leader is also the profitability leader declined from

34% in 1950 to just 7% in 2007. Just focusing on capturing the market does not ensure profits. We are living in an era where brands and businesses find it more profitable to target and serve a niche rather than service the whole market. Businesses are competing to find a profitable niche.

As a New Manager, you have moved from the midst of the action to a new vantage point, where you are able to view things from a distance. Here you can have more clarity and a better understanding of the environment in which you are operating. It's just as you might have seen in old war movies, where the General is standing on a vantage point to get a clear view of the battle. From far off, he is able to assess the strength of the enemy and its next moves, and he plans his next moves accordingly. Similarly, you have to continually assess the situations and environmental changes and adjust your plans accordingly. You have to constantly keep an eye on the operation and the environment, and fine tune your plan without losing focus on the organization's goals. The environment affecting your business includes politics, the economy, competition, the market demand, and technology. The degree of impact these factors have on your business varies depending on the size of your operation and the market in which you are operating.

With the accelerated rate of change, the need for the managers skilled enough to manage these changes is also increasing. Organizations which are not able to adapt to the changing environment are being wiped out of the market.

In this chapter, we'll discuss what the change in business has to do with the Manager aspiring to be a Corporate Tiger and why, as a New Manager, you must learn to adapt.

How Adaptability Can Help You Succeed

The politics, economics, and technology around us are changing. Businesses that are unable to adapt to the changing environment will fail. The economy is unpredictable. Things seldom go the way we plan. Technology is another factor which can overhaul the industry. Changing scenarios pose new threats and new opportunities for both professionals and businesses. The Covid-19 pandemic has derailed careers, personal lives, and businesses. Businesses and professionals have struggled to accept and adapt to the new normal. The businesses which saw this change as a growth opportunity and have adapted their operations are already back on track and are bound to sustain their losses and grow their market share.

Leaders who are short on ideas and find it difficult to respond to crises are bound to perish. Many adopt a watch and wait policy, while others look for opportunities and find novel ways to serve their customers. Organizations are investing heavily in developing virtual solutions. The goal is to create an immersive experience for their customers, adopting virtual solutions like virtual classrooms, virtual courts, and virtual exhibitions. The shares of video conferencing companies skyrocketed in these trying times. But will this trend last? Only time will tell.

The bottom line is that what you do in the face of adversity determines whether you're able to recover quickly and get back on the path to success. Corporate Tigers will identify opportunities in the face of adversity and convert them into a business proposition.

If you have a setback, do you get up and keep going—or do you need to give up and move onto something else? This is a difficult choice leaders have to make every day.

As a New Manager, learn to go with the flow. Understand that success doesn't happen overnight. You have to prepare yourself and your team to adapt to the changing professional, political, and technological environments, to help them get through failure and come out as winners. It is not just the ability of an outstanding leader to persevere, but also to know when to quit that is important. Seth Godin, in his book "The Dip," has elaborated on this concept. According to Godin, an organization doesn't fail overnight. It's their inability to sense the onset of failure that results in their disaster. As managers and leaders, we often blame market conditions for the shortfall in target or some other factor which is not controllable. But believe me, if this becomes a habit, then your failure will be inevitable. It is not the market condition, but the ability of the leader to read market dynamics and adapt accordingly, that save businesses. As a formidable leader, you do not wait for the change to happen before you adapt, but you lead the change. You are the reason for the change. For that to happen, you need to be abreast of the latest updates and news in the industry, keep innovating, and test your plans and fine tune them as you move forward. Practicing adaptability is not a one-time exercise. It is a continuous, repetitive process: lather, rinse, repeat.

The McDonald brothers, Richard and Maurice, changed their restaurant business by introducing the "Speedie Service System" in 1948. Now it's known as the Fast Food industry. In 1954, Ray Kroc joined McDonald's as franchise manager. He saw an opportunity in this new system. He convinced the McDonald brothers to sign a contract with him to expand the business through a franchise network. The McDonald brothers were process fanatics and did not want to risk their brand, so they controlled whatever Kroc did. Kroc was able to expand the business by signing in several franchises, but the money was still not flowing. The McDonald brothers were not interested in cost-saving innovations. Kroc came in contact with Harry Sonneborn, who played a vital role in converting the whole business model of the McDonald's franchise to a real estate business. They bought land and leased it to franchisees, which ensured a steady flow of income. Moreover, Kroc and Sonneborn were able to control the quality of the franchisee. Under Kroc, McDonald's became a global franchise, whereas the inventors of the system refused to adapt. Kroc forced the founders of McDonald's out of business.

Charles Darwin's theory of evolution refers to the principle of "Survival of the Fittest." It means that the species which can best adapt to changing environmental conditions are most likely to survive, while those species who don't adapt die off. That is also true in the business world, where the rate of change is snowballing. According to McKinsey & Company, 84% of executives say that innovation is important to their growth strategy, and 80% think their current business models are at risk of being disrupted soon. Airbnb, Uber, Zomato, Oyo rooms, Netflix, and many more are such business models which are technologically driven have changed the dynamics of business. Kodak, Nokia, and MySpace were once market leaders in their respective industries, but failed to adapt to the changing market conditions. Now these are either no longer in business or their market leadership is under threat.

In the last fifteen years, the music industry has undergone a tremendous change. Since the launch of Napster, the music industry responded both legally and technologically by forcing Napster to shut down its operations. However, the cat was out of the bag and, like the Hydra of Lerna, as soon as you chop off the head of one service, a new one appears. Rapid innovations have disrupted and transformed the music industry. Control over the physical distribution of the music was the deciding factor in success of the music companies, but technical innovation has changed everything. Now you don't need physical infrastructure to carry the music to customers; you can do it online. Artists and musicians don't need to run after music companies to sign contracts with them and hope for a chance to record with their label. Today, artists can record their music and release it online. This is, on one hand, an opportunity for new talent but a threat on the other hand to several businesses engaged in the music industry. The same is true for various professionals involved in the industry. The number of YouTube celebrity singers and artists is growing by the day. This competition pushes the lyric writers, singers, musicians, and composers to their creative best. This has also created demand for recording studios and opportunity for technicians and other people involved in the music industry.

This rapid transformation of the music industry is a classic example of how an innovation can disrupt an entire industry and make existing industries obsolete. That is true for all businesses and industries. The organizations and businesses which refuse to change will eventually perish, and businesses who dare to disrupt the industry norms will succeed.

Focus on long-term goals and keep tinkering with your plans to adapt to the ever-changing markets, cultures, jobs, and competition. As a leader, you are the catalyst for change. You should adapt to the environment and embrace it as an opportunity for growth rather than treat it as a threat. We know how difficult it is to make anyone change their habits, but inspiring them to strive continuously to find better ways of doing a job requires immense motivation and persistent efforts. Not only technology itself is changing, but it is also changing society, the way people think and work, as well as social and family values. In business, we cannot for sure say that nothing in the future will change. We cannot foresee that over-the-top platforms (OTT) will always stream TV, or that Google will rule the internet, or that Facebook will remain the most popular social media platform. We know these companies for their innovativeness and for their provision of spaces for boosting creativity. Yet they face challenges from lesser-known companies which pose a threat to their dominance in the industry. You just cannot afford to be complacent and bask in the glory of your past successes. As a New Manager, don't just accept the legacy systems. Challenge them! Ask the right questions and understand why the systems are in place, and where we can improve them. Outstanding leaders continuously challenge the status quo and enthuse their teams to be innovative and think outside the box.

Many people mistake flexibility for adaptability. Both of these traits are useful—related yet different. Adaptability is the ability to change to suit the environment, whereas flexibility is the ability to change or improvise without breaking the system. I'll share an example from my city. The Municipal Corporation launched a project, with much fanfare, for wet and dry garbage segregation. The Corporation distributed two bins to all the households of the city to collect waste separately. But the door-to-door collection was done by garbage collectors in rickshaws that were not adapted to collecting segregated waste. This means the wet and dry garbage were being mixed during collection, even when city residents separated them in the bins. The program had to be relaunched. They bought modified mini-trucks with separate compartments in the trunks. Since the project involved a lot of capital investment, the Corporation allotted a limited number of trucks to collect the garbage in each sector. It took more time for the trucks to collect garbage from each house. This became a problem: trucks could not collect from all the houses, as by the time they arrived, residents had already left for work. The new system is adaptable but not flexible, whereas the older system was flexible but not adaptable.

Tips for Increasing Adaptability and Going with the Flow

Some people are naturally gifted with a high level of adaptability. If that's you, then you're probably in good shape.

But what if it's not? What if you're easily discouraged or daunted by setbacks? Is there anything you can do to increase your adaptability?

Yes!

Here are some tips to help you increase your adaptability and go with the flow:

- Invest time in learning new things about the industry, business, technology, or whatever it is that interests you or applies to your workplace. Don't be afraid to apply your knowledge at both your workplace and in your life. Learning will not only help you embrace change, but prepare you for it well in advance. Knowledge of one field may also help you solve problems in other fields. Keep experimenting with your thoughts and ideas.

- Make contingency plans. You should always have a Plan B. It doesn't mean you're planning for failure. Instead, it means that you've given thought to what you'll do if Plan A doesn't go as planned. We are living in more dynamic times than ever. The markets keep changing, and if you are not part of the change, chances are that you will be left behind. In other words, "Before planning a heist, plan your escape first."

- Do away with the "we do it this way only" mentality. Learn to ask the right questions. This will give you a better understanding of the situation on the ground, and understand why the things are done, the way they are being done. In any organization, there exists a certain set of customs which many people are not willing to challenge. This results in rigidity.

You must understand not only the impending change, but also the perspectives of your team, and use your experiences and creativity to improve. The salesmen at the counter are a valuable source of information as they are the closest to the customer. They can give you ideas for boosting your sales.

- Practice resilience. Set your focus on the organization's goals. No matter how many setbacks you face, stay focused and determined. Learn to respond, not to react. Whenever you face a setback, take your time to assess the situation. Let the dust settle and then come back strong. Keep working on fine-tuning your plan. Look for the bright side and develop a positive outlook.

- Look at change as a challenge, an opportunity to learn and grow. Change is not a threat; rather, it is your fear which resists the change. The moment you transform your perspective towards change and start looking at it as an opportunity for growth rather than a threat, you will not only be better prepared to adapt, but you will be the one causing the change. An outstanding leader knows that the adage is true: "The only constant is change." You cannot fight it. You have to accept it with no limitations.

- Belief is a powerful tool. You must have a daily affirmation to remind yourself that you can deal with disappointments. Keep training your subconscious mind to believe in your goals. In the book Think and Grow Rich, Napoleon Hill suggests a detailed process of injecting both ambition and faith into your goals by repeating your affirmations every night and day. Put them in writing so that you can see them every day.

- Develop a personal process to diagnose a change and identify the challenges it will pose to your organization, to your team, and to you as a leader. Once you have identified the challenges or threats, approach them individually. Develop a game plan for each challenge and identify the key actions you need to take. Ensure that the action plan is implemented in the right spirit and keep taking feedback.

Remember that nature has allowed man to adapt to any adversity. Adversity brings out the best in us. These tips can help you learn to be more resilient in the face of any adversity. Even a big disappointment or failure will not deter you from your goals. You have assumed new responsibility and you are adapting to your new role. You are willing to enhance your efforts to mitigate all the challenges. This one change in your life has exposed you to the whole process of adaptability and helped you to develop your skills as a leader. Adaptability is a mental skill, the ability to overcome your fears and develop resilience by learning new skills and preparing for new challenges. To put it in the context of the organization or a team, as a leader, you need to help your team members overcome their fears and give them the courage to give their best efforts in the face of adversity. You must back them up when they make mistakes. Recognize the efforts by the team to do things differently even if the results are not as per the expectations. Achieving excellence requires discipline, commitment, and consistent efforts. You can motivate your team to excel, but if you don't support them in the face of failures you will not be able to develop a culture where the status quo is challenged. You cannot change certain things like market conditions or political situations, but you can change your outlook and how you approach the situation. Adapt yourself and convert challenges to opportunities like a true Corporate Tiger.

Coming up next, we'll talk about how to build a team—something that's important for every leader. Keep reading to learn more!

Skill 3: Building a High-Performance Team

****

"Coming together is a beginning, staying together is progress, and working together is success."

-Henry Ford

A team without a leader is just a crowd, and a leader without a team is a lone wanderer. It is a leader who transforms a crowd into a group, a team, a unit, and drives them towards a common goal. Team-building skills distinguish a manager from a leader. A manager only gives orders and makes team members adhere to a set of rules and guidelines, whereas a leader inspires team members to work towards a common goal and reach a higher level of success. Even the self-made millionaires out there didn't do it entirely on their own. Bill Gates is an outstanding example. Yes, he had a great idea when he created Windows—but he had a talented team of programmers, designers, writers, marketers, and administrators to help him. According to Gates, his mother was instrumental in helping Microsoft sign a deal with IBM, the deal which put Microsoft into the big league.

As a Star Performer, you are qualified and certified by your seniors. They believe that you meet a certain set of criteria, and you have now been challenged to lead a team—which may comprise of some of your former colleagues. Now, as their manager and leader, you will be commanding them, but try not to hurt their already bruised egos. New Managers find it difficult to realize that being a manager is not about authority and freedom. It is a web of relationships and expectations, full of conflicting demands, internal rifts, personality clashes, and cultural differences. The freedom of a Star Performer is entangled with dependence on the team, and the mounting targets from the seniors.

The most important role of the leader is to manage the team to deliver the results as per the expectations of the seniors. Leaders engage with their teams and channel the energy of each team member to work as one cohesive unit. Neil Armstrong, the first man to walk on the moon, would not have been able to set foot on the moon without the support of a massive team of over 300,000 people. Each person, irrespective of their title, was working with a common goal to help mankind set foot on the moon. The Romans understood the importance of teamwork. Their understanding of the power of teamwork that was instrumental in building the Great Roman Empire. They understood that a soldier standing alone with his shield and sword was as strong and as weak as the enemy soldier, but the soldiers that lock their shields together for cover on all sides are invincible.

Finding result-oriented individuals for your team is an enormous challenge, even for the best of leaders. It is even more difficult to find team players who are also result-oriented. But the most difficult task is to bind the team to a common purpose. So when recruiting, the leader has to evaluate not only the ability and skills of the candidate, but also evaluate the extent of their support of the purpose. An outstanding leader understands this concept and works with the team to make them believe that the purpose is larger than each one of them, and even larger than the team. In simple words, assimilate the team to a common faith, belief, and commitment in the objectives and goals of the organization. Irrespective of the talent and skills, if the team does not believe in the objective of the organization, they will not be able to commit their skills and talent. **Recruit Right!**

The essence of an outstanding leader is their team. To build a team, you need to incorporate a Star Performer. A Star Performer is someone who takes initiative, who does not hide behind others in the face of challenging situations, and who willingly makes an extra effort required to achieve the target. A team member who perceives change as an opportunity, not a threat, is a leader in their own right.

Each member of the team has to be developed as a leader who strives for excellence in their role. The leader motivates everyone to believe in the team as a whole, as well as to recognize the importance of their own role on the team. Managers explain the job responsibilities to their juniors. Leaders explain their roles in the team and how they are contributing to achieve the team's objectives. As a New Manager, you need to master this skill, recognize the role of each team member, and appreciate their efforts. Make your team believe they are the best at the job they are doing and that their job is important for achieving the higher purpose of the team. When former President John F. Kennedy asked a janitor working at the NASA headquarters what he was doing working so late, the man proudly replied: "I'm helping put a man on the moon." We human beings love to be acknowledged for doing a good job and being part of the bigger picture. That is why true leaders praise in public and criticize in private.

High-performance teams challenge the status quo and are not afraid to change it. They strive for excellence. Each team member has a defined role and clearly delineated responsibility. Leaders of such teams empower their team members to innovate and excel in their roles. The team members own up the responsibility to deliver results. They don't indulge in finding excuses or blaming others, but focus on results. They make their own decisions and choices in the interest of the team. Their leaders respect their decisions. But a leader cannot take their eye off the mission of the team. A leader has to support or dismiss the decisions of team members, prioritizing the larger interest of the team. **Define roles and responsibilities!**

As a leader, you are responsible for making hard decisions. Your choices will have repercussions, and may cause rifts and conflicts within the team. If you support the decision or proposal of one team member, it may not be liked or accepted by others. There will always be opposing voices, more so when the things don't go according to plan. A leader should be a master of the "art of conflict management." Conflict is a natural phenomenon in society, in organizations, and even in families. As a New Manager, you can't avoid it. You have to learn to welcome it. Conflict is an important and essential part of any team. It widens the team's perspective and provides multiple viewpoints and solutions to a problem. Managing conflict properly aligns the entire team to a common goal. A leader makes the team understand the importance of each team member's role and creates a collaborative space in which everyone believes that the overall success of the team is directly linked to their individual successes. Effective leaders must create an environment that fosters free exchange of ideas, encourages the team to speak their minds, and learns to make decisions as a team. Effective leaders use their authority sparingly to make the final call. All decisions are team decisions, made after addressing all concerns and keeping the larger picture in mind. Decisions made after collaborating are owned by the team and each individual of the team is committed. **Resolve and solve!**

For a team to work as one cohesive unit and collaborate towards the common goal, the team members should have mutual respect and trust for each other. As a New Manager, you will find that your previous track record and expertise are not enough to get you the respect and trust of your team. You have to work hard to develop powerful connections with your team members. These individual connections will help you in building a culture wherein teammates volunteer to help each other without being asked, enjoy success together, stand together in time of need, and share resources and best practices. To improve team bonds and develop a team culture, organize lunches, schedule training together, and take occasional, non-work-related team trips.

As virtual workplaces and work from home practices become more common, the challenges of leadership are increasing. This is an additional dimension which needs to be addressed. We have to prepare ourselves. I'm not saying that team members working together in concrete cubicles make outstanding team members. But face-to-face contact helps in building relations and trust, more so than the virtual sessions. Even for the virtual teams, plan one-on-one sessions. Engaging in team activities during these sessions helps in improving the bonds within the team. Team members should feel that they have support. **Help build relations and trust!**

When I look back on my experience with my bosses, the teams I was part of, and the teams where I was the boss, I see something in common: recognition. Being recognized for the outstanding work either as a team or as a team member contributed to boosted levels of motivation and cohesion within the team. A leader who rewards and recognizes their team builds confidence and earns the trust and loyalty of the team. Every time our team reached its goal, our chairperson would come personally to congratulate the team and share positive feedback. In another organization, we had a monthly reward and recognition program. The president shared the monthly team scorecard and the scorecards of the top performers before sharing the targets and plans for the upcoming month. This would set the tone for the next month. The team would be exuberant with pride.

The beauty of this powerful system is transparency. The top management clearly defines key result areas of the organization, teams, and individuals. They leave very little room for the individual biases of the managers. It is important for the reward and recognition system to be objective and transparent. A badly designed reward system can defeat the entire purpose and create bad blood between the team and organization. I have also been part of teams where leaders are more focused solely on the organization's goals and profits. They end up creating a divide between team members and standing against the team. There was little respect, and the managers had difficulty in making the team follow them. A word of appreciation and positive feedback makes it a lot easier to hear about missed targets. It is a continuous cycle, reviewing the team's performance and realigning the team to match the goals and missions of the organization. **Reward and recognize.**

As a New Manager, you have to learn to mentor and coach your team continuously. An Effective leader identifies ways to harness individual talents. Leaders groom them, like an expert gardener, so that the individuals are able to flourish and attain their full glories. To become a Corporate Tiger, you must understand that it is not the one flower which makes the garden glorious, but the arrangements of flowers and bushes. The gardener prunes and trims them to keep them healthy and thriving. The leader also keeps the team on track and shares their progress, providing constructive feedback to each member. Businesses have always witnessed change, but today, change has become rapid. We are living in an age of disruptive change. We need to build adaptable organizations. The role of the manager or the leader is to prepare their team to adapt to change and keep the team's focus and energy on track. We expect the leader to provide constructive feedback to the team to improve, excel, and prepare them for unforeseen challenges.

As a coach, you enable your team to find answers by asking questions. You don't dictate how and what to do, but help them find solutions and perform to their potential. When they are able to provide answers for themselves, the team will feel that they are involved and own their decisions and actions.

You must have heard the story of the butterfly and the cocoon. Before the butterfly can fly, it has to fight its way out of the cocoon. The struggle develops its muscles, which enables it to survive and fly once it leaves the cocoon. This is the philosophy at the heart of the coaching approach. First-time managers, whether for lack of time or to establish their authority or to downplay their teammates, resist this approach. This creates a bottleneck, as the team is afraid to make decisions and own up to their actions. They remain dependent on the leader for every decision. The Manager then becomes judgmental about the abilities of their team and tries to micromanage them. When a team member is not performing to their standards, these managers just fire and hire. They do not spend time in **Coaching and Mentoring.**

The Benefits of Building a Strong Team

Team-building is all about synergies, when one plus one is eleven. It is up to an outstanding leader to make it two or eleven. The bigger your goals, the stronger the team you need. Isaac Newton once said, "If I have seen more than others, it's because I have stood on the shoulders of giants." To cut a long story short, you cannot succeed without a team. As a manager, you are leading a team, and you are responsible for the team's achievements. As hard as you might try, no matter how determined you may be, you cannot do everything on your own. It is not practical, and it's not working smarter—it's working harder.

Consider the phrase, "jack of all trades, master of none." You might be great in some roles, but chances are there are some skills in which you are just average (or below average). If you put your hand in those areas, you may hurt your business or your position as a leader. Behind every successful business, sportsperson, or organization is the team and its sacrifices, commitment, and loyalty. It is the team that provides your organization its hard-to-beat competitive advantage.

The team should bring in diversity and creativity. It provides you with the flexibility to do what you like most and use yourself to the best. It is normal for a manager to be tempted to putting their hands in everything which involves their team. As a first-time manager, you may be tempted to do it yourself to get the work done, but my advice is to avoid this temptation. As a leader, your plate is already full, and you should focus on doing more valuable activities. Build connections and bond with your team, and do not micro-manage the team. Make yourself available when they need you, and avoid looking over their shoulder. Don't lose sight of the bigger picture. Set milestones and review with your team. Take ideas, don't just give orders. First-time managers tend to make this mistake, and end up feeling frustrated that they are not yet ready for a bigger role.

The trick, of course, is building the right team. I will share some tips I learned from my bosses. I've applied these and shared them with my teams over the last twenty years:

- Yell for Help and Run to Help
- Do It Right the First Time
- Strive to Outdo Yourself
- Share Best Practices
- Convince or Get Convinced

Yell for Help and Run to Help

This is a basic principle of teamwork: it's all about helping each other. If, while doing your work, you realize you will fall short of your target, yell out for help. Don't wait until it is too late. The moment you hear such a call, be the first to extend your support. Each team member is a link in a chain. One weak link can jeopardize the entire project. The underlying spirit is "one for all and all for one." You should be ready to extend support to your teammates. You should be a whistleblower when things don't go as planned. Don't wait for someone else to discover the problem. If you notice something, be the first to volunteer and fix it.

Do It Right the First Time

Take an extra hour or day to complete the task, but make sure it is right, and be sure that you have given your best shot. The cost of mistakes and rework is heavy. The cost is not only monetary, but the non-monetary costs are difficult to reimburse. Losing time in redoing work not only derails the team, it costs the team its credibility.

Strive to Outdo Yourself

Every day, you should approach your work with a goal to do better than yesterday. You're in a competition with yourself. Act as though you are the best person for the job, and then beat yourself at it. As an expert, you should find ways to do the task more efficiently: use fewer resources, finish in less time, or make the process foolproof.

Share Best Practices

As they say, nothing succeeds like success, and your success motivates your peers. Never hesitate to share your ideas and the best practices you adopt in following the principle of striving to outdo yourself. As a leader, create a formal platform to share best practices within the team. It will energize your team, and you will achieve extraordinary results in a much shorter time.

Convince or Get Convinced

This is a little tricky. It has to do with the trust and relationships between your team members. Many organizations and their teams work as a set of individuals. Each one has a chip on their shoulder. They discuss issues not to resolve them, but to judge others. Such dysfunctional teams are destined for failure: they are the problem and never a part of the solution. An articulate leader will be able to identify the concerns of the team members and guide them towards a solution. Such leaders understand that each team player has to be fully committed to ensure team success. Before the team decides, the issue must be debated and discussed thoroughly. A passionate debate is essential for any team, be it your family or profession. This we have already discussed earlier in this chapter: the leader has to Resolve and Solve.

Tips for Attracting Team Members and Knowing When You Need Help

You need a team, but where do you start?

The first step is identifying the key values and principles you stand for, as well as the values that drive your organization and your customers' expectations. Once you identify these values and principles, they become a beacon for making hard decisions at all levels of the hierarchy. We cannot teach values, but you can teach skills and choose a team which shares your values. Values are like the string that bind all the beads of a necklace. When you share the same values and principles, it becomes easy to set and achieve goals no matter how difficult they may seem.

The next step is to identify the areas where you need support or the things that aren't in your wheelhouse. Maybe you have little marketing experience or you're not good at organizing. As a first-time manager, you may or may not get the chance to hire or select your team. But be sure that you have team members who can help you with your weaknesses. You'll have the best chance of success if you use this method.

To do that, you'll need to:

- Write accurate and attractive job descriptions. These are brief and include: clearly defined skills required to do the major functions of the job; a suitable job title; and potential growth path for the position. Involve your team in writing the job descriptions for each team member. The one you already have may not reflect the realities of the job. This exercise will help you to clarify the roles of each team member and also address any gaps in the team's skillset.

- To attract and retain good talent, you must ensure a fair wage. The payment structure should be intrinsic to the productivity and the growth of the organization. Attractive pay packages attract good talent, but to retain them, you need more than a good pay package. Be open to hiring an employee on a part-time basis if the cost of retention is high.

- Nowadays, many organizations encourage their employees to recommend to them the right talent for the vacant positions. Share the job description with the team and your contacts to ask them to recommend the right talent. Employee referral programs are much cheaper and more efficient than any other source of recruitment.

- Advertise and market your vacancy using the right marketing tools. It is difficult to find the right talent. Marketing tools such as job portals and Linkedin can help carry your message to the right people. Do some research on which marketing tools will be most suitable to carry your message to the right people.

- Interview people with the objective of finding out if the candidate has the right attitude and qualifications for the job. Remember that you are there to interview and not to interrogate. Listen more and talk less.

Make sure that you ask for samples of their work where it's appropriate and check their references. These days, it's easy to hire people to work remotely without ever meeting them. You should set up virtual interviews with anyone you cannot meet in person.

It's also a good idea to impose a probation period on any new hires. You can also try out assignment-based employment by attracting talent from platforms like Upwork and Freelancer. That way, you'll be able to make changes easily if you need to. Just put everything in writing.

Next, we'll discuss strategic thinking.

Skill 4: Strategic Thinking and Planning

****

> *"Strategic planning is not strategic thinking. Indeed, strategic planning often spoils strategic thinking, causing managers to confuse real vision with the manipulation of numbers."*
>
> *-Henry Mintzberg*

New managers, and even experienced ones, confuse strategy, strategic planning, and strategic thinking. All three are related yet different. Strategy is a summary of action plans which will take you closer to the organization's vision. Strategic planning, however, focuses on defining the strategy and committing your resources. As part of strategic planning, a leader has to decide where to commit or not commit resources. Strategic planning is distinguishing between what you will and won't do to achieve your vision.

Strategic planning has a long-term effect on the health and future of the organization. It affects limited resources and their utilization. Strategic planning is required not only for business organizations, but also for public sector undertakings where there is a shortage of resources. The government annually allocates funds, and departments receiving these funds compete for larger shares of the budget. Leaders of these organizations focus on making maximal impact with minimal resources.

Strategic thinking, on the other hand, is the mental process of analyzing critical factors and variables on which the success of the organization depends. It is required at all levels in the organization. Strategic thinkers are required to make, implement, and run their strategic plans successfully. In the constantly changing landscape of financial and political uncertainty, where the expectations and demands of the customers are fickle, it is critical for the leader to strengthen strategic thinkers at all levels. The environment, economy, politics, and technology are changing faster than ever before, so it is up to the frontline executives to be in constant touch with the customers and market trends. They need to be empowered to fine-tune their strategies at the time of execution to achieve the vision and mission of the organization. With the changing trends, organizations have realized that they need to adapt fast, and to adapt fast they should be lean. The concept of lean was first implemented by Toyota, which primarily is a customer-focused approach of reducing waste from the organization processes. According to lean philosophy, any activity which does not add value to the customer and for which the customer is not willing to pay is a waste. The success of Toyota inspired many organizations to adopt lean management. The leaders of lean organizations make a conscious effort to reduce the hierarchy levels within the organization so as to remain close to their customers. This enables them to respond quickly to customer demands. Any critical information about changes in the market reaches the top quickly, and decisions are conveyed faster. This enables organizations to create and respond to the change quickly. Organizations build agility to adapt to market conditions and other environmental changes. Moreover, organizations cannot be expected to make quick decisions without developing the strategic thinking skills at all levels. As a New Manager on the way to becoming a Corporate Tiger, you have to constantly keep working to improve your and your team's strategic thinking. It is the ability of the individual to foresee the impact of decisions on the internal departments, customers, and competitors of the organization not only today, but also in the future.

As per Harvard Business Review, strategic thinking is the single most important leadership skill. It has been found in their research that it is

10 times more important to the perception of effectiveness of leaders. It is also a difficult skill to acquire, as it is more of a mindset than a set of techniques. As a strategic leader, you should understand how your role and the department's role impacts the organization's long-term goal. You must also make your team understand their roles. This will help them empathize with management and will help them make informed decisions. The organization's vision and objective has to be spelled out in clear terms so that each member of the team understands. It becomes the common goal of the team. With each step they take, they should believe they are closer to achieving their dream. Any divergence is not just reported, but comes with a plan to put the team back on track. The team will also understand the cost of sacrificing short-term gains to achieve long-term objectives. A proposition may sound very lucrative in the short run, but if it does not align with the long-term goals of the organization, it is prudent not to invest time and resources into it.

Strategic thinkers focus on creating innovation rather than just competing for control of the market. You create uniqueness in terms of the quality of services you provide, and the way you do business. This will help you in creating an advantage which will be difficult for the competition to replicate. I'll share a personal anecdote.

Me and my wife were constructing our house, doing rounds of the market to buy the building and hardware material. I believe we must have visited over a hundred hardware stores in town. It was not just the best price that we were looking for, but also the best quality. During our search, we came across an impressive hardware store. It's like any other hardware store, but what impressed me most was the customized service they offered. The transparency in the cost of the accessories and well-defined systems are remarkable. They make their customers feel comfortable and important. The customer experience we got in the store was unmatched, especially compared to the stores dealing in building material. It is a lean operation, difficult to duplicate. The store's quality of service assured us that the quality of material would also be good.

Successful leaders create an interesting value proposition for customers. As a strategic thinker, you should create a value proposition for each product your organization sells, for each market segment the organization caters, and for the brand itself. As a first-time manager, your first challenge is to create consistency of service/response in the department's operations for your internal and external customers. You do this by identifying and creating the value proposition. It can be in terms of the process or protocol to be followed for any complaint or service request regarding the process in which your team is involved.

The breed of strategic thinkers is far more difficult to find than one would imagine as it is the most difficult skill to develop. Strategic thinking requires you to solve not only today's problems, but also tomorrow's problems. It is a skill that needs to be built up within the organization and injected into its DNA gradually.

In their book Leading with Strategic Thinking, Aaron K. Olson & B. Keith Simerson explain that strategic thinking is at the intersection of three fields of study: cognitive psychology, systems thinking, and game theory. Cognitive psychology (the study of the mind and how it processes information) encompasses perception, problem solving, creativity, learning, thinking, and memory. It focuses on finding the dots. Systems thinking is connecting these dots and understanding how they relate. In this context, systems thinking is understanding how the ecosystem of the business works. You must have heard about the butterfly effect. The theory was first proposed by Edward Lorenz, who said that the flapping wings of a butterfly in the distance can influence the formation of a tornado at some other place. The focus of systems thinking is to establish the cause-and-effect relationships between various factors. In the current business scenario, the importance and complexity of systems thinking has increased multifold. The factors are constantly changing, and so are their effects on businesses.

You must have filled out a customer feedback form at one time or another. Nowadays most of the organizations are collecting these forms as a fad or to pose as a customer-centric organization. But organizations which seldom process feedback forms or do not have the proper processing system for feedback miss out big time. The feedback process is not limited to processing. It starts from the point it is collected. The time required to fill out a feedback form should be incorporated into the budget, as well as the time required to process the feedback. The process owner has to be sensitive about the need for and importance of the feedback and should not force the customer to give feedback. But a true customer-centric organization will not just depend on these feedback forms or customer surveys; they will constantly strive to find opportunities for improvement from the customer complaint data or other market reports. Opportunities can also be found in the competitors' reports! The manager may ignore a stray complaint about a process, but that complaint may highlight a larger underlying issue which may affect the long-term prospects of the business. The ability to identify and relate such issues distinguishes a Manager from a Corporate Tiger.

The third dimension of strategic thinking is game theory. Game theory proposes to integrate the element of competition into the strategic thinking process. The environmental changes and the analyses and understanding of the interrelation of different factors are important, but the other players in the market are also responding to these changes. Their adjustments will have a direct bearing on an organization's performance and long-term existence. Each player will plan their own strategy and brace for the impact of these factors on their respective businesses. When you are running a marathon, you maintain your speed and save your stamina and strength while also keeping an eye on the other runners. A slight stumble can cost you the race. Similarly, strategic thinkers always keep tabs on what their competing brands are doing. For the micro-, small-, and medium-sized enterprises, it is always a challenge to collect reliable and worthwhile market information about competitors, and leaders seldom invest their energies in finding out about the competition.

In 1994, Henry Mintzberg wrote that strategic thinking is more about "connecting the dots" than "finding the dots." It is about combining personal knowledge, experience, and market information to find a path that the organization should follow to achieve its objectives. It is an essential skill, required for strategic planning to be successful. We require strategic thinking to keep the plan on course, to develop strategies, and to execute it.

Strategic Leadership and Strategic Thinking

A strategic leader is one who drives the organization's vision and mission and keeps the ship on course amid political, economic, and market changes. Strategic thinking is a skill which enables managers or leaders to plan with an end in mind and to remove the hurdles that come along. It is an essential skill a leader must develop to lead their team.

These turbulent times test the strategic thinking skills of the leader. Chaos shows the true character of the leader. People look up to you to guide them through troubled waters. Strategic thinking will help you build a plan of action to drive through, and strategic leadership will make the team believe in you and follow you. When things are not going as planned, your leadership will be doubted and challenged. Leaders are always blamed for crises. Your strategic thinking will help you establish your credibility and authority as a leader. A leader of any organization has to respond to:

1. Technology and Innovation
2. Economic Environment
3. Customer
4. Competition

The composition or impact of these elements on an individual business will be different. They may have an immediate effect or a long-term effect. Strategic thinking is a far more complex skill than the other skills we have discussed so far, as it includes a combination of several abilities and skills. Let us try to understand the various ingredients of strategic thinking before we dig into developing and improving it. The skills which are important part of strategic thinking are:

1. Critical Thinking, Analytical Skills, and Problem-Solving Skills
2. Systems Thinking
3. Aggressive Listening
4. Management and Collaborative Skills

Critical Thinking, Analytical Skills, and Problem-Solving Skills

Every day at work, you are facing one problem or another, irrespective of your position in the hierarchy. These problems require you to analyze the data thrown at you, process it, and convert it into meaningful information for you or your senior to act on. As a first-time manager, it is you who are required to come up with alternate solutions, critically analyze these, and choose the best alternative. As you rise through the hierarchy, the problems that knock on your door grow more complex and stretch your critical thinking and analytical skills. Your team will expect you to provide long-term solutions to these problems. They expect you to fix the issue so that it does not crop up again and the organization remains on course to achieve its objectives. It is a linear approach to problem solving. As a strategic thinker, you must understand and analyze the data, study the patterns, and forecast future trends.

Systems Thinking

We are living in a world that is more interconnected than ever. We interact with various systems daily, without ever realizing the complexity and interdependency of these systems. Systems thinking is an ability to see how the systems around you work and how the business ecosystems interconnect and depend on one another. The human body is composed of several systems, such as the respiratory system, digestive system, nervous system, and muscular system, with each system having its own role. All these systems work both independently and together to make the human body function. As a first-time manager, you should understand the several information systems working independently within your organization. There are marketing and sales management systems; then for manufacturing organizations, there is a production system; operations for service organization; there's research and development; and then there are financial and bookkeeping systems, human resources, supply chain management, information management, and business intelligence. If anything goes wrong in any of our body's systems, the systems transmit a signal to the brain, which has the ability to evaluate the response and take corrective action. This is crucial. It is how you know to eat when you are hungry and to sleep when you are tired. If you ignore the signals, you become sick. Similarly, the systems operating within the organization and the systems with which these systems interact outside the organization provide feedback and response. Strategic thinkers set up their own feedback system to capture signals. Then they try to establish a cause and an effect, just as a doctor diagnoses and treats a patient. The strategic thinker also establishes the cause-and-effect relationship in the long term as well as the short term for each decision before implementing it, and also analyses its impact on other systems within the organization. Systems thinking focuses on finding out whether a political upheaval or environmental catastrophe in one part of the world is likely to affect your organization or not. A ripple created in any part of the business system will either become a tsunami or will it correct itself. As a leader, you need to understand the cause of the ripple and prepare for the impact before it hits you. You may run your business in a politically stable country, but if your customer base is in a country at war or facing civil unrest, your business is going to take a hit, and so are your suppliers, unless you find an alternate market.

Aggressive Listening

A strategic thinker is not just a listener, but an aggressive listener. As an aggressive listener, you welcome—even invite—criticism of your ideas. You help people around you to open up and share their own thoughts and ideas. You involve the team in the decision-making process and include their perspective in policy-making and strategizing. As the old adage goes: "You have two ears to listen and one mouth to speak." A strategic leader understands this well. You need to learn to ask the right questions to get the right answers. By giving 100% of your attention to the speaker, you not only show that person respect, but also gain the confidence of the speaker. We see this also in our personal lives: if we are not attentive to our children or our spouse, it creates mistrust and often causes irreparable damage.

In professional life and for strategic leadership, one needs to be an aggressive listener. As an aggressive listener, you not only listen to and interpret the speaker's words, but also empathize with and connect emotionally to the speaker. Even if you miss the words, you will not miss the emotion. Words are used to convey the need or requirement; emotions convey the underlying feelings that have resulted in the need. If you can address the emotions, you will win the loyalty and trust of the person. Visionary leaders are always looking to win the loyalty and faith of their followers.

Management and Collaborative Skills

The best of plans unimplemented will fail, and the worst of plans will work with proper implementation. To implement a plan, you need the commitment and collaboration of a team. Once you decide the strategy, the time has come to implement it. I have come across many first-time managers who struggle to implement plans, due either to a lack of management skills or an inability to harness the support of their team. You will require management and collaborative skills for successful implementation and execution of the strategy. You should determine the key expected results of a successful implementation of the strategy. You should clearly communicate the key result areas to your team.

As business operations become more complex, the traditional hierarchical leadership models are being replaced by flattened hierarchies and lean organizations. The focus is on using the collective intelligence of the team to solve the complex problems facing the organization. It's about breaking down silos and putting the best team players to work on the bigger and complex problems. The ability to plan and collaborate across hierarchies and departments ensures we implement the strategic plans across the entire organization and that the management is not struggling against internal resistance to change. The leader has to keep a firm focus on the overall vision and mission of the organization and not deter from it despite the challenges.

Tips for Improving Your Strategic Thinking and Planning

Some people have a natural gift for strategic thinking. They're the people who are skilled chess players and who seem to see ten steps ahead. If you're not one of them, don't worry. Here are some tips to help you improve your strategic thinking. Strategic thinking is a skill, to be sure, but like any skill, you can cultivate it. If you'd like to build your workforce into a team of long-term strategic thinkers, here are some pointers to get you started:

- Each decision and action has a consequence. Give yourself time to think through the decision strategically. Don't make decisions based on your gut. Train yourself to listen to the dissenters and accept their views as a new perspective. Make data-driven decisions. Before you finalize a decision, ask strategic questions, and encourage your team to do the same and collect as much information as possible analyze it before committing. This exercise will help you develop your planning skills and help you identify new opportunities. Strategic questions can relate to business opportunities, feasibility of an idea, whether a plan aligns with the organization's vision and mission, product launch or entering a new market, restructuring the organization, tackling the competitors' strategy, or any other aspect of the business.
- Question everything, find answers, and see ideas objectively. Think critically about your goals and work backwards to figure out what actions will help you achieve them. Analyze the current situation and work forward to identify the steps you need to take and the gaps you need to fill. A sound strategy has strong analyses and facts at its foundation. Instead of just working with assumptions, collect information and use it to draft your strategy. Perform IF-THEN-

ELSE IF analyses and use a mix of reverse-engineering and forward engineering to develop a strategy. Develop statistical models and use simulations to test your strategies.

- Involve team members, trusted friends, and industry experts for suggestions to help you plan strategically. Improve your listening skills. Listen to your team. Their thinking may be flawed, but it will give you a fresh perspective. Attend conferences, seminars, and workshops to get a fresh perspective and capture contextual information. Consider opposing ideas so that you don't overlook any possibilities. Seek information about the market, competitor, customers, and innovations in the industries related to your business. Share the information with your leaders and team. This will help them to have a broader perspective.
- Be patient and receptive to the trends both inside and outside the organization, and within the industry and related industries. Regularly invest in learning the development in the world economy and other developments in fields that will affect your business model. Be conscious of the actions being taken by your competitors and other industry leaders that negate or take advantage of the changing environmental

conditions. Keep your team updated on the internal developments in the organization.

- Set a timeline for each goal post on your way to achieving your success. You can set a yearly plan for implementing the strategy and then break it into a quarterly, then monthly, then weekly plan. Sit with your team for at least fifteen to thirty minutes at the beginning of the week and talk through the work that needs to be done in the next few days. This will help you in breaking down the yearly goals to monthly plans and weekly actionable tasks.
- Choose a mentor with good strategic thinking skills, and encourage team members to do the same. You may request your seniors or colleagues within the organization to mentor your team members.

The more you practice strategic thinking, the easier it will be. You can improve your strategic thinking skills at your own pace. You can also pursue various training exercises to help you improve your strategic thinking skills.

Coming up next, we'll talk about the fifth and final must-have leadership skill in this book: delegation.

Skill 5: The Art of Delegation

****

"Delegation requires the willingness to pay for short-term failures in order to gain long-term competency."

-Dave Ramsey

Delegation, the process by which the leader shares authority and distributes work to the team, is essential for effective management. It is one of the most essential leadership skills. I believe all four skills of effective leadership are connected to delegation. It is the heart and soul of good leadership. You build a team (Skill 3) so that you can give them tasks which will help you attain the organization's vision and mission. Once you delegate, it will free you to devote more time to strategic thinking and planning (Skill 4). You need to be an effective communicator (Skill 1) to assign the tasks and pass on the instructions in a way that drives results. Tailor your leadership style and supervision to each team member and the tasks at hand (Skill 2). Your team members will work on different tasks requiring diverse skills. This will allow you to develop your team's distinct skillset to adapt to upcoming challenges.

The ability to delegate will have a lasting impact on the success of the organization. It is this skill which truly focuses on utilizing the most important and complex resource at your disposal: the people who are part of your team. Delegation frees the leader to focus on a common goal while the team takes care of routine activities. It also helps in keeping the team motivated and helps them grow. Leaders cannot and should not do everything by themselves, as they have to lead and manage. As a first-time manager, the shift from "doing" to "making others do" is the biggest transition in your career and part of becoming a boss. Your ability to delegate will determine the future course of your career. Understand that your job is to manage, not execute. That is why you are a manager.

A manager achieves the department objectives by planning, managing the people, and using other resources. As part of planning, the manager decides what is to be done and who has to do it so that the department objectives are met in the most efficient way. Delegation entails two aspects: one is the assignment of the task; and second is the assignment of authority to the person assigned the task. It is this second aspect which makes it rather tricky to select the right person for the job. There are several myths and fears in the minds of first-time managers which may prevent them from delegating effectively. The key to learning how to delegate effectively is understanding why even seasoned managers sometimes hesitate to delegate tasks. As a Star Performer, you have enjoyed the freedom of doing the job, and as a New Manager you have to give the same freedom to your team. You cannot get carried away with your authority and stifle the creativity of the team by micromanaging their activities. You should avoid becoming a helicopter parent to your subordinates. Give them the freedom to do their jobs, but be available to them when they waver. You have to keep them on track. For that, you should develop a feedback mechanism.

Remember that when you delegate, you do not delegate responsibility. In other words, you can transfer your work, but not your responsibility. Since delegation does not mean transfer of responsibility, the manager and leaders resist delegating the work. If they do delegate tasks, they do so without giving the employee the proper authority, not realizing that that defeats the entire purpose of delegation. The tasks, instead of getting completed in less time, are further delayed. And, despite the leader distributing the work, the routine and mundane activities take up much of the leader's time. It's fear of failure and lack of confidence in the team that prevents such managers from distributing their tasks and authority. This fear leads them to delegate the same task to two different people to ensure that the task is accomplished, resulting in the waste of time and manpower. The hesitation to delegate results in confusion, chaos, and frustration within the team and organization.

You may hesitate to delegate because you feel you will lose control. And if you lose control, your position is jeopardized. Such leaders often distribute their work, but do not transfer their authority. Imposing their authority can never earn the respect of their subordinates. You should realize that by delegating, you will not be losing control, but will instead prepare yourself for a future role with even more responsibility. Delegation will also help you gain confidence and respect for both your subordinates and bosses. If your team is performing well with minimal input from you, you will have more time at hand to take up other important tasks. One of my mentors gave me this guidance: you should spare yourself so that you can do/understand the jobs of your boss and your boss's boss so that you can succeed them when the time comes. Similarly, groom your successor by delegating tasks to your juniors; as you do this, you will also develop skills to succeed your boss. When the opportunity comes, you can present yourself as a replacement for your boss, and you will have prepared a replacement for yourself as well.

You may decide not to delegate a task just because you love doing that task. You may be very good at doing a particular task and believe that no one can do it better than you. This is an implicit barrier. It is a function of human psychology that we delegate the work we don't enjoy doing. We assign the least desirable tasks to a young recruit and reserve the more favorable tasks for ourselves. In one of the organizations I was working with, I noticed in the accounts department that every time a new person joined they were immediately given the job of cashier. Everyone in the department hated cashiering, as it involved commuting to the banks and handling all cash transactions. The job was important, but due to the labor involved in executing the job, the team members avoided it. And the new recruit would sooner or later succumb under the pressure of managing cash. The department would then be back to looking for a new recruit. No one actually tried to provide support or resolve the situation.

As you rise through the organization, it becomes a habit, this clinging to tasks you just love doing. In the process, you lose the opportunity to discover other important tasks which may interest you. If you allow yourself to settle into your comfort zone, you'll stop growing. When you become a manager, you are observed by both your team and your bosses. If you're not careful, your complacency will spread to your team and even throughout the entire organization. Remember that you can enjoy your comfort zone but cannot grow in it, and when you stop growing, you die. Delegate the tasks which others can do, or the tasks which are too easy for you.

Affordability is another reason managers are unwilling to delegate. They feel that hiring outside help will be costly, and they prefer to do the job themselves to save money. But because they do not factor in the costs of doing it on their own time, they lose the benefits of hiring an expert. An expert will not only do a better job, but will also do it in less time. Affordability is not just about monetary compensation, but also the time you spend on getting the job done. It is better even if you have staff available to you, but know that you can occasionally outsource the work. It is better to outsource an activity if you do not have the required skillset or if time does not permit anyone on the team to finish it due to any prior engagements.

In small organizations, the manager may also feel that their team is already too busy and additional tasks will just increase everyone's workloads. So the manager might end up doing it on their own. Delegation is not just distributing the work to your team, but also outsourcing. Look for an agency which can take care of your work in a cheap and efficient way. Many organizations have a strategy to outsource the bulk of their operations and concentrate only on business development and marketing. Bharti Airtel had adopted this strategy, where it outsourced its core operations and worked as a Telecom Marketing agency. But, with the changing business environment, they reworked their strategy and started shifting core operations in-house.

There are people unwilling to delegate because they think, "I will complete the task by the time I explain the task to someone else and train them to do it." If you are one of them, then believe me: it is the effort of training that you are resisting, and it has nothing to do with the effort or time needed to do the job itself. You don't realize that you may do the task now, but when it has to be done again, you may have neither the time to do it yourself nor a person trained to do it. This means that either you will not complete the job, or you will do it at the cost of some other more important job. So, as a manager, by making excuses you have lost an opportunity to train and develop your team. Not only this, you have also lost an opportunity for personal growth. If you keep doing what you already know, then you will never be able to spare yourself to learn new skills. You need to gain more skills to accomplish the more complex task of strategic planning.

You might be very efficient at doing something, but when you have to delegate, don't micromanage. Just let your subordinate do it. They may not be efficient at it in the beginning, but they will find their own way to accomplish it. As a first-time manager, you might be tempted to exhibit your skills. If you micromanage, you will kill the creativity and innovation of your team. Keep experimenting, and don't be afraid of failures—and don't let your teammates be afraid of it, either. Your fear of failure will not let you share authority. You assign the task, then micromanage it, give detailed instructions, keep following up on it, and finally end up doing yourself. It is this fear of failure that prevents you from trusting your team. This fear is infectious. Your subordinates will avoid making decisions, leaving everything up to you. As a leader, you have to support them and make them accountable for the results even though you are ultimately responsible for the results. Start thinking like a mentor and coach: make yourself available to the team when they need you, but do not pester them by asking for frequent updates. Give them clear instructions and agree on the frequency of review and milestones. Encourage them to innovate, and come to you with solutions, not problems. You yourself have to be part of the solution, and not a problem.

Because of these various mental blocks and fears, managers may delegate the work, but they delegate it without following the principles of delegation. In this chapter, we'll talk about why delegation is important and provide some tips to help you delegate the right tasks to the right people.

Why You Shouldn't Try to Do Everything Yourself

An outstanding leader is not the one who knows everything and does everything, but the one who knows how to delegate tasks and is the best person to do the task. But before we get into that, let's understand why you should not try to do everything.

I have come across energetic managers who involve themselves in everything that goes on in the organization—even routine administrative tasks and activities—without realizing the risk of burnout. It's good to be involved in things concerning your organization, but it is better to be involved with the people in the organization. Involve yourself in coaching and mentoring the people doing the job rather than doing their jobs for or with them. Take care of your people; people will take care of the job.

As a leader or manager, you handle the most important and expensive resource of the organization: Human Resources (i.e., the people reporting to you). It is your responsibility to use them to get the maximum return on the investment in this asset. As a leader, if you don't delegate, you will end up underutilizing this resource and overloading yourself. This puts you at risk of burning out. Delegating properly will have a positive impact on the employees, the leaders, and organization. Let me list these advantages of delegation for employees:

1. Empowers employees
2. Develops New Skills
3. Increases Accountability
4. Encourages Prioritization

We can also examine the impact of delegation on the leader:

1. Develops Leadership Skills
2. Develops New Skills
3. Increases Influence
4. Restores Energy

And, of course, delegation's impact on the organization:

1. Encourages a Culture of Innovation and Creativity
2. Effective Management and Builds Trust and Commitment
3. Facilitates Growth and Leadership Succession

Impact of Delegation on Employees

Empowers Employees

When you delegate a task to an employee, you are also confirming their ability to take up the task and be responsible for the results. By delegating a task, you also delegate the authority to make the decisions required to complete the task at hand, which makes them responsible for the results. This helps them to understand both their importance as a team member, and the importance of the team overall. By delegating, you also invite your team to be a part of the larger picture. This will encourage commitment and engagement.

Develops New Skills

When you delegate, you give employees an opportunity to grow their skills. The task may require them to learn a new skillset. If the employees are involved in the same activities again and again, they tend to become complacent. So, as a manager, keep challenging them by upsetting the status quo. Challenge them to accept additional responsibilities and motivate them to develop new skills. When you delegate properly, you also set the tone for building a higher level of competency in the team. Delegation may require the individual to be trained in the new process, interact with other departments, or interact with the suppliers or customers. This will help them improve their communication skills, interpersonal skills, and team-building skills.

Increases Accountability

Delegation involves your subordinates, makes them feel important, and shows your faith in their abilities. You not only transfer the task, but also the authority and accountability (although, being the supervisor, the responsibility for the results remains with you). You share the responsibility and accountability with your subordinates without actually absolving yourself of it. Your boss will hold you accountable for the result, not your subordinates. So, it is important that you hold them accountable also and develop your system of supervision and monitoring.

Encourages Prioritization

Time is of the essence in any activity, and that is the exact reason you need to delegate. You will always have tasks with conflicting deadlines, so it's important to decide which tasks to finish first, and which you should or should not delegate. How do you organize priorities? Steven Covey shares Eisenhower's time management matrix, which helps prioritize your tasks and responsibilities. There are four categories in which you can place all your tasks:

Quadrant 1: Urgent and Important

Quadrant 2: Not Urgent but
Important

Quadrant 3: Urgent but not
Important

Quadrant 4: Not Urgent and not
Important

We will discuss this matrix again when we discuss how to delegate.

Impact of Delegation on Leaders

Develop New Skills

By delegating, you get more time to lead and coach your team, as well as do strategic thinking. The concept of delegation is founded on the necessity of leveraging the time of others. So when you delegate, you learn new styles of supervision. This is important because while one method of supervision may work for some, it may not be as effective for others. There will be team members who need fewer follow-ups and directions, and there will be some who need more of your supervisory time. As a leader, adjust your style to be effective. This will help your communication skills, team-building skills, and, above all, your supervision skills.

Increase Influence

As a first-time manager, you need to increase your influence. It is your influence which impacts the character, behavior, and motivation of the team. It is the power to change the course of action without any apparent or direct effort. Delegation is a powerful tool for a leader to increase their influence. When you delegate, you place trust in your team. Trust is a two-way street: you give trust to gain trust. When you delegate a task, you not only demonstrate trust, but also make your team member feel important. They will not let you down if you sincerely believe in their ability and make them feel important. They will trust you, be ready to move mountains at your command, and make you a formidable leader in the long run. The increased influence will help you put strategic plans into action, make new initiatives a success, and bring about positive change in the organization.

Restores Energy

Delegation helps you achieve more in less time by leveraging the time of others. It will help you use the skills and abilities of your team and give you more time to spend in rejuvenating your energies. The entire purpose of delegation and sharing the responsibilities is to get more time to focus on more important things at work and in your life. These are things that help you reduce stress and rejuvenate your mind. A healthy mind will be more productive and efficient.

Impact on Organizations

Encourages a Culture of Innovation and Creativity

As I mentioned earlier, managers drive the performance of the most important and complex resource of the organization: Human Resources. It is the skill of the leader to delegate that will make work exciting for the team. If not done properly, the team may feel that the manager is just offloading their own work onto the team. In this case, the work will be taken as a burden rather than an opportunity. Delegation done properly will push people to raise their bar, challenge their creativity, and draw them out of their comfort zones. New challenges will break the monotony and ensure the team is not complacent. A new task and activity will excite them and make them use new skills. If you keep working on the same set of skills, it will do more harm than good. Untapped skills and talents will never be discovered if employees don't have the opportunity to exercise them. Delegation is an effective process not only to tap skills from the source, but also to help employees evolve. When you involve people in problem solving, you get more solutions and less resistance to the implementation of change. You will find alternative ways of doing the same tasks, leading to improved productivity and efficiency.

Effective Management and Builds Trust and Commitment

Effective delegation leads to team-building and faster results. The improved productivity will result in higher profits and higher growth. Everyone wants to be a part of a growing organization. Fast-growing organizations attract and retain better talent. When you delegate decision-making, you empower employees to fix things faster, which in turn leads to shared responsibility and stronger commitment. Organizations with committed manpower are able to resolve customer complaints faster. This helps you earn the trust of your customers.

As a manager, you trust your team to make decisions for you; moreover, as a leader, you get committed people working for both your success and the success of the organization.

Facilitates Growth and Leadership Succession

Delegation is the easiest and most inexpensive method of training and developing your team's skills. Delegation also helps you to test how an individual performs under pressure and whether they are ready for the next level. With proper planning and management, through delegation you can build a second tier of leaders who are ready to take up more responsible positions. This gives the management the flexibility to focus on growing their business and improving efficiency and productivity.

Tips to Help You Decide What to Delegate to Others

Planning is the starting point for any activity. Because delegation requires a lot of planning, be clear about the objective of the task or job being delegated. The leaders who cannot plan their delegation are the ones who find themselves stuck performing routine activities. They are busy fighting the everyday fires. A good leader understands this and creates a system of delegation which explains the desired results and objectives of the job, what will determine its success and failure, the frequency and timing of reviews, and expected milestones to be covered between reviews.

As a leader, you must decide 1) what to delegate; and 2) who to delegate to.

What to delegate?

As a manager and leader, you will always face these questions: What should I delegate? What should I do on my own? There is no ready-made formula which can help you make this decision. This skill you will learn over time, but one thing you should keep in mind while delegating is that you do not delegate responsibility. You share it. This may make you uncomfortable in the beginning and make it difficult to delegate. There are various theories that propose which tasks should be delegated. Some of the more common suggestions by various authors and leaders have been listed below:

1. Tasks of repetitive or mechanical nature
2. Tasks which do not involve any decision-making or which require simple decisions
3. Time-consuming activities
4. Jobs that require skills you are not good at
5. Things that are not defined in your job description

You can start by asking a few questions:

- What are the things that your team members excel at?
- What are the things you can teach them to do?
- What are the things that don't require your personal input?

It might be useful to start by identifying the things that only you can do. These may include making strategic decisions about your team or meeting with investors. Then, make a list of the things you can delegate.

Brian Tracy, in his book Delegation & Supervision, has elaborated on the subject. He proposes the Factory Model of Management to aid your thinking and improve your productivity and results. You consider each team member, each work unit, each department as a factory, where you process inputs to achieve a specific output. As a leader, you create a charter to define the expected results of each individual department and work unit. Determine the key result areas for yourself as a leader of the unit, department, or team, and also identify key result areas for each teammate. Use measurement-based management. This is a philosophy propagated by the Quality Gurus in the post-war era, which helped transform Japan into an economic power. It is based on a simple principle: "What we cannot measure, we cannot improve." It is important that we translate all business activities into quantitative and numerical terms. Once the individual knows the parameters used to measure their performance and the metrics being used to measure performance, they will strive to improve it. As a first-time manager, you should focus on understanding how these metrics align with the organization's goals.

In his book, Tracy also discusses two other powerful management techniques for delegation: 1) Management by Objective, and 2) Management by Exception. While Management by Objective focuses on empowering the employees, Management by Exception is a method of control. To use the Management by Objective method, you set long-term objectives, agree on the desired results with your team, give your team freedom to use their creativity, and give them the skills and resources to achieve them. You build a system of regular evaluation. In contrast, the Management by Exception method is a control tool. The team must report any exception or deviation from the set path to the leader. This saves the leader a lot of time and does not require their involvement in routine or daily firefighting activities.

Delegation is associated with saving time for the manager/leader. The aim of delegation is effective management and time utilization by the manager. Eisenhower's Time Management Matrix, as described by Steven Covey in his book The 7 Habits of Highly Effective People, helps a leader or manager decide which tasks to prioritize based on the importance and urgency of the task at hand.

This is an effective tool meant to focus the attention of the manager on tasks that matter most to your business and personal growth. Eisenhower's Time Management Matrix provides a roadmap for managers to decide what they should delegate and what they should not. The matrix has four quadrants:

	Urgent	Not Urgent
Important	**Quadrant I** • Crises • Processing problems • Deadline driven projects	**Quadrant II** • Relation building • Finding new opportunities • Long-term planning • Preventative activities • Personal growth • Recreation
Not Important	**Quadrant III** • Interruptions • Emails, calls, meetings • Popular activities • Proximate present matters	**Quadrant IV** • Routine Tasks • Time wasters • Repetitive Tasks • Some calls and emails

Quadrant IV: Activities categorized under this quadrant are not important and not urgent. And you do not need to be a rocket scientist to know that these activities should not be on your to-do list. You should delegate them and move on.

Quadrant III: In this category are activities which are not important but are urgent. They are unavoidable. They are perfect candidates for delegation to employees needing to brush up on their skills.

Quadrant II: We have a category for tasks which are not urgent but are important. The leader should focus the most of their time and energy in dealing with these tasks. A majority of leaders do not spend sufficient time on the tasks and activities in this quadrant. Rather, they wait until these become crises and move up to Quadrant I.

Quadrant I: This quadrant is the source of much stress. Tasks and activities categorized here will always eat up the time of the leader. The best way to avoid dealing with crises is to address them while they are still in Quadrant II.

A New Manager may struggle to identify Quadrant II activities. In the popular television series Suits, the director has beautifully portrayed the new manager's dilemma. In Suits, a newly appointed Managing Partner, Louis Litt, struggles not only to delegate but also to supervise. Louis is afraid to delegate, and when he does delegate to new partner Alex Williams, he gets jittery as the deal with the client gets bumpy. It tempts him to take things back into his own hands without giving Alex an opportunity to fix it. He does not bother to listen to Harvey Spectre, another name partner in the firm, who is a star performer and Louis's idol and co-worker before promotion, when he suggests a risky solution for the problem. This solution eventually leads to risking the very existence of the firm. This is the kind of situation you will face as a leader every day. Maintain balance and trust your teammates to come through, but do not leave everything to them. Think through the ideas and plans before executing them.

According to Mike Michalowicz, a leader is engaged in four phases of activities: Doing, Deciding, Delegating, and Designing. He suggests that the ideal mix for a leader should be 80% doing, 2% deciding, 8% delegating, and 10% designing. Note that he suggests that the deciding phase should only be at 2%, which means your subordinates do not take up all your time. You empower them to make decisions and fight the daily fires on their own. Your focus should be more on doing the most important tasks on which the survival of the company depends. You are the one designing strategies to build a stronger business.

Michalowicz calls this important activity the "Queen Bee Role," or "QBR," in his business book Clock Work. The role of the Queen Bee in the hive is to reproduce, giving birth to the next generation of bees. Similarly, the role of the business leader is to generate business, grow revenue, and ensure the financial viability of the organization. In order to fulfill the QBR, managers must identify the one activity on which the success of the company depends. He suggests a simple process to identifying this one activity:

Step 1: You need at least six sticky notes. You write one job on each sticky note, totaling six. These tasks could be daily, weekly, monthly, or annually. (These are primarily Quadrant I and II activities.) Write the things that, according to you, matter the most for the business.

Step 2: Place all the notes in a line in front of you and jot down the time you spend on each task in a week.

Step 3: Now identify tasks from the list which you can drop by either improving the systems or by delegating or outsourcing, until you have two tasks left.

Step 4: Choose a task which you will never let go, the task which you yourself must perform. This task is your number one priority. This is your QBR.

Once you identify your QBR, you arrange the sticky notes so that the priority is in the center, and all other tasks placed in a circle around it. This should represent a wheel, with the QBR representing the hub. A task that takes more time to complete is placed farther from the center, whereas a task taking less time is placed closer to the QBR sticky note. We then join each non-QBR task to the center with a straight line, so that the lines represent the spokes of a wheel. Now list all the other activities from Quadrants I, III, and IV, along with the time they consume, and place them within the wheel. Now you have a visual representation of your activities.

You probably, at this stage, have an unbalanced wheel. But not to worry! We can balance the wheel. Start with the longest spoke and determine whether you can trim it (shorten the time being spent on the activity), transfer it (delegate it), or trash it (avoid or eliminate it). Finally, you will have a QBR wheel similar to the one below, where you have identified the activities you need to Delegate, Avoid, and Reduce.

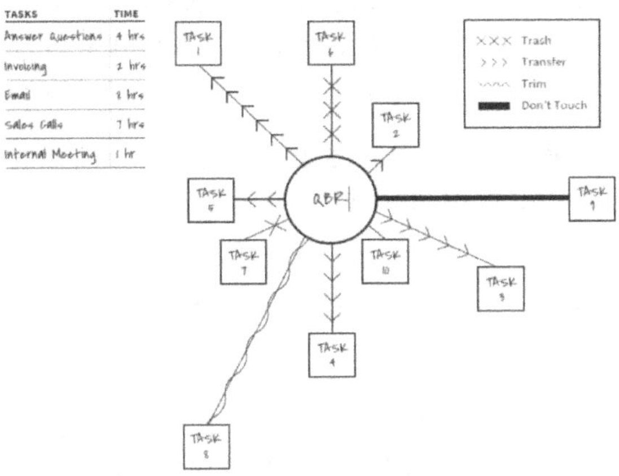

This exercise will definitely help you identify the activities or tasks which should never be delegated and which tasks do need to be delegated. Now that we have identified these, the next step is to identify the right persons to take on these responsibilities.

Who to Delegate to

Once you've identified the jobs you have to delegate, it's time to think about who are the best people to be doing the jobs. Let the individual decide the job. Forget what each person was hired to do. Try to find the underlying skills and the natural talents the person possesses. Here are some questions to ask:

Which team members already have skills that make them suitable for the task?

Which team members have shown an aptitude for core skills, such as communication, teamwork, or logic?

Which team members are eager to learn and willing to take on new challenges?

The answers to these questions will lead you to the right people on the team to whom you can delegate the task.

Another important aspect to consider is whether the activity should be done with in-house or outsourced talent? You may have the talent in-house, but it may be cheaper or faster to get it done by an outside agency. If the activity is a one-off and not likely to be repeated in the near future, you may get it done by talent on platforms like Upwork or Fiverr.

Once you've identified the people you need, spend some time thinking about the training and support they'll need to succeed in their delegated tasks. You may need to spend some one-on-one time with them or pay someone else to train them. They may need an outside class or seminar.

Make sure that you communicate clearly about what you expect from each team member to whom you've delegated tasks.

Decide with them a schedule for reviews, what will be included in the reviews, and what will determine success or failure.

Make yourself available to answer questions, and keep in mind that they may not get it right on the first try. There's a chance that you may need to adapt along the way. You might not pick the best team member for every task on your first try. The key is to keep an open mind, to listen, and be patient.

In the words of Richard Branson: "Train the people so that they can leave, and treat them well enough so they don't want to." You'll need all your leadership skills to decide what to delegate, to choose the best people for each job, and to guide them along the road to success. That's why I saved the art of delegation for last–it's a skill that incorporates all the other skills we've discussed.

Final Words

Thank you for reading From Star Performer to Corporate Tiger: 5 Key Skills to Succeed for New Managers. I hope you've found the information in this book to be enlightening, useful, and inspiring. This may be the end of the book, but it is the beginning of a new journey for you as a first-time manager. The definition of leadership is changing along with the times. It's not just limited to the title and position you hold in the organization. In the words of Abraham Lincoln: "Whatever you are, be a good one." I believe that is the whole spirit of leadership, and that is what you should expect your subordinates to be. As a leader, you want to select the best of the available recruits; as an employee, you want to work with the best organizations. The skills that we have discussed are in no way conclusive skills of leadership, but they are important. These are skills which, as a first-time manager, you must master in order to grow.

Here are some core concepts to remember as you practice your leadership skills:

1. Practice communication at all times and be willing to learn from your mistakes. Remember that in all communication, you should do it with clarity, detail, and

honesty. Communication is not a one-way but a two-way street; it is your responsibility to build a conducive environment to make it happen. Work on your listening skills and build trust. Learn to address problems rather than react or respond. As a first-time manager, you must learn to effectively communicate the objectives, goals, and key result areas to your subordinates, and to assert your opinions and ideas to upper management.

2. An outstanding leader is not one who digs his heels in and refuses to budge, but one who can assess the situation and adapt accordingly. Depending on the situation, you may be required to lead from the front or from afar. Your ability to adapt and make contingency plans will always help you stay one step ahead. In times of crisis or when things don't go according to plan, people will look to the leader to steer them clear of the situation.
3. Leaders become great because they build talented teams. Without a team, there is no leader. A pack of wolves can beat a tiger any day, even though a lone wolf cannot match the strength of a tiger. Build a team where each team member complements and provides synergy for the team. As a first-time manager, you also have to learn to manage the conflict within the team.

The key is to identify the small irritants at the initial stages before they blow out of proportion.

4. Like in a game of chess, the leader has to think strategically and plan his moves, keeping in consideration the competitors' moves. Remember, each action has consequences. An excellent leader thinks of the consequences before committing to any action. Strategic leaders always keep one eye on the organization's goals and identify the practical steps they need to take to achieve them. The other eye is on all other forces, such as market conditions and economic and technological development. As a strategic thinker and leader, it is all about making choices and clarity. It is a tradeoff between long-term benefits and short-term gains.
5. Delegation is the skill that will ultimately determine the level of success you can achieve. As a first-time manager, you must learn to trust your team to do the work for which you are responsible. Delegation frees you to strive for the next level. You must learn to identify the tasks which need your attention, and which can be handled by your team. If you delegate well, you will be able to achieve more in a shorter time. You will deliver results, while other managers struggle to get going.

> Select the team members best suited to each job, train them well, and leave them to find their own ways, monitoring them regularly to keep the ship on course.

Leadership is not a riddle to be solved. It's a skill—or rather, a set of skills. These skills can be learned and mastered by anybody who is willing to do the hard work. Remember, it is your hard work and skills that have helped you reach where you are today. Practice the skills you have learned in this book and keep your heart in the right place. Build relationships, but not at the cost of authority. As a leader, you are not only influencing, managing, and coordinating with people down the line, but also with people who are not directly under your chain of command.

Learning is a continuous process. As a manager, you should always invest your time and energy in learning and improving your skills, as well as the skills of your team members. The more skilled your team, the more productive and reliable their work and results.

The five core skills I've described in this book are the basis of great leadership. As I mentioned, you have begun a new journey by reading this book. Now you should not rest until you achieve your goals. I believe you have taken the first step to becoming an outstanding leader and are well on your way to becoming a Corporate Tiger!

Good luck!

References

Introduction

https://hbr.org/2007/01/becoming-the-boss

https://www.chieflearningofficer.com/2018/03/21/follow-the-leadership-spending/

https://thomasplummer.medium.com/why-young-managers-fail-600dfb9e89ea

https://www.pradco.com/developing-leaders/top-3-reasons-new-managers-fail/

Communication Skills

https://gatewaytolearning.osu.edu/leadership-development/building-relationships/communicating-as-manager/#:~:text=Communication%20is%20the%20heart%20of,and%20sharing%20information%20with%20people.

https://strengthscape.com/essential-communication-skills-for-new-managers/
https://www.managementstudyguide.com/difference-communication-and-effective-communication.htm

https://www.hvst.com/posts/learning-from-wal-marts-sam-walton-wBqTRpY1

7 Habits of Highly Effective People by Steven Covey
https://www.ccl.org/leadership-solutions/leadership-topics/leadership-and-communication-skills/

https://www.ccl.org/articles/leading-effectively-articles/communication-1-idea-3-facts-5-tips/

https://www.ddiworld.com/blog/the-state-of-frontline-leadership-in-2020

Adaptability

https://hbr.org/2011/07/adaptability-the-new-competitive-advantage

Dip by Seth Godin

https://en.wikipedia.org/wiki/McDonald%27s

https://www.mckinsey.com/business-functions/strategy-and-corporate-finance/our-insights/innovation-and-commercialization-2010-mckinsey-global-survey-results#

https://en.wikipedia.org/wiki/Lernaean_Hydra

https://en.wikipedia.org/wiki/Music_industry

https://www.businessnewsdaily.com/10157-resilience-adaptability-business-success.html#:~:text=Business%20is%20constantly%20changing%2C%20and,and%20maintaining%20a%20positive%20attitude.

https://hbr.org/2011/07/adaptability-the-new-competitive-advantage

Team Building

https://hbr.org/2007/01/becoming-the-boss

https://hbr.org/2019/11/the-leader-as-coach

Develop your leadership skills by John Adair

https://vouchforme.co/great-examples-of-teamwork/

COACHING FOR LEADERSHIP by Marshall Goldsmith and Laurence S. Lyons

BUILDING A HIGH-PERFORMANCE TEAM by Sarah Cook

The Five Dysfunctions of a Team by Patrick Lencioni

https://www.naukrirms.com/blog/why-employee-referrals-are-the-best-source-of-hire/#:~:text=Employee%20referrals%20are%20the%20candidates,them%20monetary%20or%20other%20rewards.

Strategic Thinking

https://cmoe.com/glossary/strategic-thinking/#:~:text=Strategic%20thinking%20is%20simply%20an,a%20team%2C%20or%20an%20individual.

http://www.strategicthinking.eu/5-reasons-why-you-need-strategic-thinking-on-all-levels-of-your-organisation/

https://hbr.org/2014/02/develop-strategic-thinkers-throughout-your-organization

https://en.wikipedia.org/wiki/Cognitive_psychology

https://thesystemsthinker.com/wp-content/uploads/2016/03/Introduction-to-Systems-Thinking-IMS013Epk.pdf

https://thesystemsthinker.com/introduction-to-systems-thinking/
Systems | Free Full-Text | What is Systems Thinking? Expert Perspectives from the WPI Systems Thinking Colloquium of 2 October 2019 (mdpi.com)

https://en.wikipedia.org/wiki/Strategic_thinking

https://hbr.org/1994/01/the-fall-and-rise-of-strategic-planning

https://online.hbs.edu/blog/post/how-to-develop-strategic-thinking-skills

https://online.hbs.edu/blog/post/how-to-develop-strategic-thinking-skills#:~:text=Strategic%20thinking%20skills%20are%20any,or%20even%20years%20to%20achieve.

https://matterapp.com/strategic-thinking/

Delegation

Delegation and Supervision by Brian Tracy

The Leader in You by Dale Carnegie

https://www.livemint.com/Companies/v0BPytPnOJMAalnMRWRDAM/Bharti-Airtels-evolving-outsourcing-strategy.html

Clock Work by Mike Michalowicz

7 Habits of Highly Effective People Steven Covey

for more resources

Visit: www.manusharma.live

https://career-boosters.teachable.com/

www.ingramcontent.com/pod-product-compliance
Lightning Source LLC
LaVergne TN
LVHW020642100826
845148LV00012B/2304

* 9 7 8 1 6 8 5 6 3 8 2 4 5 *